When Summer Ends

Scarlett Olacsi

BookLeaf Publishing

India | USA | UK

When Summer Ends © 2024 Scarlett Olacsi

All rights reserved.

No part of this publication may be reproduced, stored in a retrieval system, or transmitted, in any form or by any means, electronic, mechanical, photocopying, recording or otherwise, without the prior written permission of the presenters.

Scarlett Olacsi asserts the moral right to be identified as author of this work.

Presentation by *BookLeaf Publishing*

Web: www.bookleafpub.com

E-mail: info@bookleafpub.com

ISBN: 9789360941499

First edition 2024

PREFACE

I told myself I wouldn't write about you anymore...

But I did.

(Sorry.)

If I Had Never Met You

Life goes on like it always did
Always does, I suppose
An average day -
And I stand at the bottom floor of a local
supermarket
Picking up a few things for dinner with my
mom.
a place like this is not for an adventure, you'd
think
I don't either
But upstairs
I see a blonde haired boy
With headphones
And a hoodie
Messing around with his friends
A curly haired brunette -
Eating unicorn cake, of all things
How fun it would be to be there, I'd think
To have friends who don't all live far
To share a piece of cake with
And a few jokes --
Deja Vu
But for something I've never experienced
For a friendship I've never had
For walks past curfew

For shooting stars I've never seen
For music I've never heard
For road trips I've never planned
Fairs I've never been too, prizes I've never won
--
And I stand there for a moment,
As I watch him glance at me
From the corner of his gaze and
For a moment I think he recognizes me
But the next he turns away again
And life goes on
Like it always does.

Artemis

16
And we sat on the play structure
Watching shooting stars go by
My first one ever
I saw with you
Nearly a year later
We're sitting beside one another
This park is much bigger
I watch city lights and pretend
There are stars in the gray sky
And how could everything change so much?
I think of summer and how I miss it
I think of us and watch a photo album
Flipping pages
Where we came from
What we've become
You breath out smoke
That matches this evening light
Your eyes don't seem as blue in this moment
I sit myself up
Let my feet hang off the slide
And I hug you
If only I could stay here forever
But like Artemis
We hold on tightly to the string of our bow

Then all at once, we have to let go
To let our stars
Shoot across our skies

When Summer Ends

Summer will be ending
And everything will change
School will start
And leaves will fall
And I'll be alone once again
After summer ends
Does that mean you will leave me?
Does that mean no more climbing trees
Or meeting every evening
Will you be so busy
You forget my name
The way it sounds on your tongue
I guess you can't be blamed
"No one will forget about you, "
 you hold my hands strong and tight
I wish I could believe you
But I worry about this every night
When summer ends
When sweat and heat cease
The scrapes and bruises finally heal
On my arms and knees
When every day becomes a blur
When I don't wear your hat anymore
And your ring
falls off my thumb for the last time

When summer ends
I will be alone again.

I never live when I mean too.

I'm not an impulsive person
When I stood in an empty parking lot
No ride,it was dark outside, I stopped scrolling
on my phone and I stared at your name
I should've called you.
But I never live when I mean to.
Tonight I talked about you with my girl bestie. I
read her a poem I wrote.
She said, you know, he's at work right now.
It was true - your red car in the parking lot.
We could drop by, if you want, she said.
You could say hi.
It's been six months.
So?
No.
I never live when I mean too.
I have a menagerie of paper memories.
A paper strawberry garden like the one your
father said he was going to plant that summer,
and call it "Scarletts strawberry patch."
I have paper figures of a princess in a prom
dress, and a boy that looks kinda like you if we
had gone to prom together last may.

On your birthday, we stood in the soda shop,
waiting for drinks and my favorite song came
on.
I asked you if you wanted to dance.
You said, not here.
That's what we have in common, you and me
We never live when we need to.

Adventure

Take me on an adventure
I'd follow you anywhere
To hell
Through barbed wire fences
steep hills
Rocks beneath our feet
Cramps in our sides
I'll follow you when it's dark out
My mind grasping on to the outline of your body
All I can see in this darkness
Take me on an adventure
Under bridges we once danced under
On paths we've walked again and again but
never on this night
Just hold on, you say
I'm holding on to all the good moments I can
think of
And here tonight I would sit here with you
forever
Until it was pitch black and past curfew
Holding on tightly to all of this
Take me on an adventure
I'll pretend the smoke is just our breath
Visible in the cold air
As I watch your chest rise and fall

And your evening eyes set
I'll pretend
It's summer again
And we will go on another adventure soon
I'll pretend
I'll hold on
Take me on an adventure.

Warm Rain

Let's spend the day in the city
Eat lunch as we walk along the greenbelt
Drink monster as we blast music under bridges
That we've stood under time and time again
And slowly, warm rain starts to fall
This summer has warmed even the clouds
And my cheeks are painted
with the same red I see
As the sun falls
Now, orange cream drips from the sky
Rain blurs the hues of coral and gold
As the night closes in,
I feel safe in the light of the sunset
How lovely it is,
To hide behind the horizon
If it can hide the sun
It can hide me
How lovely it is
To spend this day with you
Dancing in the warm rain
How lovely it is to know
You have lived today

Maybe.

I went to Wendy's the other day, for a
peppermint frosty
It's that time of year again, so I thought I'd get
in the spirit
My dad wanted to go inside, so I walked in with
him
And I saw your little brother.
His hair is long now. He had it up in a ponytail.
He was with his friends, laughing and smiling.
He glanced at me, but looked away, didn't say
anything. I wonder what you've told him.
I wonder if he'll tell you, when he gets home.
If we were still friends, I would have waved at
him
Nodded at him at least
We'd at least acknowledge each other
But you're the boy who broke my heart
I'm the girl who used to come over everyday
A couple years ago, your best friend
If I were 16 I'd smile at your brother
I'd say, hey, issac
He'd say hi
And explain to his friends
Say
That's just my brothers friend

It's weird, I write stories about you still
I talked with one of our mutual friends the other
day
I asked him if you would have come
If I called you, that day when I needed someone
He said, maybe
He'd maybe, probably pick up, at least
That's not the answer I wanted to hear.
I wanted him to say yes, he would come.
Yes, he would drive and pick you up, when you
were there, in the dark. He would come for you.
He would come to your rescue. In a heartbeat, he
would come, because he loves you.
But it was a maybe.
And that's not enough for me.

Our Summer

14

I'm supposed to burn easily, yet
My skin only softens in the heat
The humidity drains us as we walk
Slowly
sun beating down on us
But
I would not rather be home
I wouldn't it rather be winter
I want to stay right here in our summer
Where I can feel free
And warm

All my friends will one day be strangers

All my friends will one day be strangers
Midnight parks and traffic cones nothing but a
memory
You won't remember the time I ran after you
So fast I tasted blood in my mouth
Will you forget me, I asked?
Time will only tell, you reply
One day we will have
Different lives with different lovers
We'll be graduated and have our last summer
Where we spent our days drinking lemonade and
monster
Exploring the town we've always lived
My friends will one day be strangers
I'm writing poetry in Paris and
You're across the world
We'll stop walking home every day
One day
All my friends will be strangers

16 in the Summer

I'll never be
16 in the summer
Spinning down the street in your ripped up
hoodie
Never be
Walking around town
Going nowhere
Just wanna be with you
I'll never be
I'll never be
I'll never be 16 in the summer

We met at a carnival
Winning prizes, taking me above on a ferris
wheel
I can see the whole town from here
The place I've always lived but I never had
You
I never had this moment before
16 in the summer
Never felt so magical
We fake fought with golf clubs
And you taught me how to swim again
I faced every fear with you
Never been so adventurous

I miss the the me I was when I was
16 in the summer

I climbed trees and you always gave me a boost
Catching me before I fell down
I remember chasing after you
After a fight and crying on the sidewalk next to
your house
I'll never be
16 in the summer

And when it all ended
When our friendship fell apart
When we started growing up before we had too
I still miss that summer
I miss strawberry blonde and
Red caps and golden rings
I wish I could be
I wish I could be
I wish I could be 16 in the summer

City Lights

We sit above the city lights
And listen to the songs that remind me of you
In my mind I'm holding your hand
In my mind there are stars in our eyes
And you love me
And everything is coming back to me
Everything I wanted but ignored because of her
The butterflies in my chest
The memories of you I've held in my heart
And I want to be friends
I want to learn everything about you
I want it to be like it was before
We sit above city lights
I think of a life that could have been mine
And you are so excited about the stars
I love how excited you are about space
And music
And I want to dance with you
Even though I'm scared
Even though the dangers of loving cross my
mind
I want to sit here forever
In this moment
Looking at the sparkling city
The one we grew up in

As our hearts broke
And then learned to love again anyway
I think that's what living is supposed to be like
And I know I'll go home soon
I know things will stay the same as they are
But I'll always have this moment right
Part of me is always going to love you
And I hope we can find what we're meant for
But it would be nice
If we could do it together
We sit above city lights
I want to stay here
For a thousand years.

Epilogue

It was dark outside in the city
And I was alone
His car not in the place we parked this morning
Called him and called him
No reply
And as I went through my contacts
Standing there in the parking lot
My eyes stopped on your name.
We haven't spoken in 5 months
I wonder if I called you
Would you come?
Would you pick up?
Would you be mad?
You used to come to my rescue
Would've called you without hesitation
If I were still 16
But I stare at my phone
In the dark
In the parking lot
Then I scroll past your name
I guess things are not the same anymore
I guess if the world was ending I would not
come over
I guess if I was dying on my knees
If I was in the war zone

And there was no one left to call
I guess that I would just die
I guess I wouldn't say goodbye
I guess my eyes would scan the room for you
But if they found you
I'd look away
I guess after all we had been through
I would stand in the dark
In the city streets
All by myself
Listening to police sirens
Laughter and cat calls
Honking cars
Sniffing cigarette smoke and rain
I guess
I am too proud
To even forgive you
For survival
For self preservation -
If there was an earthquake I wouldn't ask if you
were okay
When your dog died I lingered on your profile
And erased messages
I'll never send
Don't know if I'm too proud
Or just ashamed
That I ever loved you enough
For it hurt this much
I guess this means I don't love you anymore

I guess
The last page has been turned
And there is no epilogue
For us.

Mad Inside

They say you should never date a person in your
friend group
Because if you break up you break up the whole
group well it's true
Used to spend our lunch period together while
you guys smoked in your car
Now I only still talk to two of you
And on Tuesday it's our best friends 19th
birthday
I wanna go but I know you'll be there
I know him better than that, know he'd forgive
me if I didn't come
But I still feel guilty for not being there
So I texted you late said I'm not even mad
Don't wanna be friends, don't wanna date you,
don't wanna play you, but can we please be
acquaintances again and you texted back
quickly, said I'm lost, but sure, Merry Christmas
The mistletoe wilted in that moment
Yeah merry fucking Christmas
To tell you the truth it made me angry, made my
cheeks turn red
I deleted our conversations and all the things I
said

I don't know what I miss when I think about
you?
The attention you never gave, all the times you
didn't come through
I've written novels of poems that are just about
us
but you're not worth all those words I wrote for
you
I don't know why I ever tried
I just miss what could've been
Say it could've been you
But we're not in high school no more
I'm growing up
you're still in the same old dark lonely place
I'm working hard, you still sit in your car
smoking
I've heard you said that you messed up too badly
this time
Well it's true and I take it back
I'll always be mad inside.

Best Friend

Every once in awhile
I check that playlist that you made for me
To see if u added anything
You want me to hear
Almost called you in the dark on Wednesday
I was scared and then thought of you
The parking lot was empty and it smelled like
cigarettes
Every once in awhile
I imagine you show up my school
Ask to talk to me in the hall, you pull me aside
and say
I still think of you
And you go on to say
every once in awhile
I consider showing up to your house
See if you'd want me or if you'd tell me
To go fuck myself
know I hurt you know I played you
Wanna say that I'm ashamed you
Ever cried on my account
And there's a million ways I could respond
But I don't know which scenario will play
Cuz I wrote you poems, wrote you texts
That I erased

Because
We were best friends once
We were 16
Against the world
Pink converse against blue marshmallow dreams
And every once in awhile
I put on your hoodie, I kept it
It's an awful orange, too big on me, but it
reminds me of how things used to be and
I miss my old friends, i made some new friends
but they don't know who I am, who I'm not,
where I've been,
Every once in awhile
I ask about you and I wonder if you do the same
for me
Kinda hope you do
Kinda hope I mattered somewhat to you
Every once in awhile
My eyes rest on your name, or photo , and I
think
Goddamn
They taught me about heartbreak
But they never once say how much it hurts
When he was your best friend.

1,2,3

Things change
And I'm trying to be okay with that
I hoped that as they changed
Our grip would be firm as stone
But things change
And as you wriggle your hand out of mine
I see the scars I've left on your wrist
And the rope burns on my palms
and people feel like balloons
Like balloons you must grip onto so they don't
float away
That's how it's always been for me, my grip hard
in desperation
that no one would leave me again
but the string is long since worn
and you turn away from me and
I understand what my words that night really
meant
and so you float
And drift away
In and out of reach
Gradually becoming higher and higher until I
cannot see you at all
And though my eyes will fill with tears
Though my balloon is stuck on the ground

I'll fill it up with air best I can
And maybe
Somewhere in space
Among the stars, I will find you again
And you'll let me squeeze you one last time
1,2,3, I Love You
Becomes 1,2,3 I Let Go

Friends

"Forever,
Is a false construct,"
I told you
Came right out of my own mouth
Nothing lasts forever, nothing
I suppose I just didn't expect
It all to end so soon
Please forget
Something
In my life
And come back for it
Please, please
I just wanted to be your friend
What you are to me is
My best friend and
No one ever told me how much more painful it
is
To lose someone who knows
Everything about you and
They say friends don't destroy one another
What do they know about friends?

Forever

Remember that time in September
We walked home
I showed you the abandoned train and you
watched me climb it
I asked you to leave
You wouldn't leave
You yelled
That's why I won't leave!
Why won't you leave?
Because it's not a thing a good person would do
And you are a good person

So I came down
And you stuck by my side when I needed you
But when you carry something for a long time
You get tired
And more tired
And more tired
And 130 pounds became
A thousand
So of course you had to leave
And you try to make it better now
Tell me you're around if I need you
I wish I could trust you

We haven't talked about anything real for a long
time

And I liked the idea of a best friend and I
thought sometimes if we'd ever be something
more
Because I knew that look in your eyes
I knew there was a bigger reason you were
trying so hard
When you met her it was a chance
An escape
A time to move on
To find a new center
Of the world and
Sometimes I want to be 16 again
Just to feel something twice
Feelings never make sense
Is it possible to love
Could I be in love
With multiple people
And you were my second home
And I miss that so damn much
And it needed to happen but how I wish it didn't
happen
Remember strawberry chocolate cake and no
bake cookies and gingerbread
Gingerbread will always remind me of you now
I prefer to think of all the happy parts
Not when everything ended

And I felt safer in your bed then I did in mine
I felt more like me when I was by your side
And there are two lies everyone always wants to
believe:
1. There is a such thing as forever
2. I will be lucky enough to have forever
I hope never to be fooled again
But I will.

Park

We sat up on the play structure
Right next to the slide
In a couple of weeks
They would tear it all up
You slid down with ease
Sitting on top of our pasts
Gesturing to me at the bottom
I hesitate, holding on
Are you really scared of slides? He said
You need to come down either way
You need to come down
And I let go
A grin on my face as I go down
Just like that, it's over
And we're walking home
Never to see that park again

It Snowed Today, I Thought of You

It snowed today, I thought of you
Cold white fluff in strawberry strands
I thought of all the things I wish I could tell you
Though I know if I did
You wouldn't be as excited as you would be
When we were 16
If I could talk to the you back then
I wouldn't speak of our friendships fall
I'd talk of high school graduation, my first
semester of college
I'd speak of poetry, I'd tell you about our friends
baby
How we're all grown up
And I might tell a lie
That we still talk
That I fell in love
So you don't have to give up after all
You once told me you liked me and part of you
probably always would
Well I'd say that's good
Because I still think of you
In everything I see
I think of you when I'm in an empty parking lot

Scrolling through my contacts, stop at your
name
But I do not press it
I don't call you
Even when I need you
Though I would never tell you
And when it snows, when the music plays,
little things like blue skies and rain
I still think of all that I would say
If I could go back
I would smile
And I'd hug you
Before the moment ends
Before the years go by
Before we grow up and grow apart,
I would squeeze your hand three times
I would look into your evening eyes
I'd admit it if I could
That after all this time I've cared about you
After all the time I denied you
Now I'm older and I've grown up and know
better then to text you late at night
And wait for you to respond in morning light
That It snowed today, and I thought of you
And how I still love you
Ain't it the worst thing you've ever heard?
That I love you
And if I know you at all
You'd shake your head and smile

no you don't, you'd say
You'd never believe me when I used to say
So I squeeze your hand 3 times
Look into your evening eyes
And say
It snowed today,
I thought of you.

I Wish To Lie Here Forever

I wish to lie here forever
To dig myself a grave to sleep
Let flowers grow over my body
Let my blowing hair become blowing grass
Overgrown
And beautiful
A place where
No one will hurt me
A place where
No one will think to look
Where all the hardships of the world fade away
as I become ash and dust
I wish to lie here forever

Summer

I met you in May
I spent my days alone
I didn't talk much
Used to loneliness
That didn't seem like loneliness any more
So much as
My normal life
You sent me a message
And I said hi
Then we were talking every day
Throughout the day
And it feels strange
To have someone that says good morning every
time I wake up
And goodnight whenever I'm ready to sleep
Someone who knows
What I did today
How I felt
We met at a park
In the dark
I don't leave the house much but
I walk you to the flagpole and say words I never
have before
Swearing down the street
I cry in front of someone

I spill my secrets
I don't know if you're easy to talk to
Or if I've simply been so desperate
For human connection
I can't control myself
And suddenly
I'm adventurous
I'm not alone
I hang with you
More than I'm alone and
Self isolation seems painful now
When it wasn't before
Because now I have best friends
Now I have someone to call
When I'm crying
When I am bored
or happy
And even if
You were to leave me
Before summer ends
I'd look back and think
That was,
A hella good summer
Even if
Summers never the same again
It could be my new favorite season
All cuz one year
I was able to spend it with you.

www.ingramcontent.com/pod-product-compliance
Lightning Source LLC
La Vergne TN
LVHW010924200726
843509LV00013B/2064